Just Call Us Lucky

Wesley F. Buchele

Additional copies of this book may be ordered from Shires Press, Manchester Center, Vermont:

(802) 362-2200

1-800-437-3700 (toll free)

www.northshire.com

Just Call Us Lucky

A Kansas Farm Family
During the Great Depression

By

Twins Luther and Wesley Buchele

Wesley and Luther at age 3 in 1923.

SHIRES
PRESS

4869 Main Street
P.O. Box 2200
Manchester Center, Vermont 05255
www.northshire.com/printondemand.php

Cover by Heather Bellanca
Front cover photo credit (hay bales in background): http://scott.liddell.com
Back cover photo: Twins Wesley and Luther Buchele at the age of 81,
when they started writing their memoirs. Photo by Heidi Buchele Harris.

ISBN: 978-1-60571-012-9
Library of Congress Control Number: 2008907123

Building Community, One Book at a Time
*This book was printed at the Northshire Bookstore, a family-owned, independent bookstore
in Manchester Center, Vermont, since 1976. We are committed to excellence in bookselling.
The Northshire Bookstore's mission is to serve as a resource for information,
ideas, and entertainment while honoring the needs of customers, staff, and community.*

Printed in the United States of America
using an Espresso Book Machine from On Demand Books

Contents

Preface   *vii*

Acknowledgments   *ix*

Introduction   *1*

The Linchpin: Mother Bessie (1883–1981)   *6*

Charles John Buchele (1873–1931)   *11*

Robert Leroy (1904–1986)   *16*

Charles Ned (1906–2000)   *20*

James Paul (1913–1992), the first of the "great brothers"   *23*

Julian Milton (1915–1983), the second "great brother"   *27*

Matthew John (1917–1983)   *31*

The Twins: Luther Holroyd and Wesley Fisher (1920–)   *35*

Photographs   *59*

Mother Bessie Buchele with her seven sons in 1958. *Top L-R:* Matthew (Dr. of Medicine), Ned (Farmer), Wesley (Prof of Ag. Engineering), Luther (Student Co-op Exec. Sec.). *Bottom:* Paul (Farmer), Robert (Dr. of Osteopathy), and Julian (Farmer).

Preface

As our older brothers have passed on, we twins, the last survivors of the large Buchele family of Cedar Vale, Kansas, understood that if a history of our clan were ever to be written, we would have to do it. To our regret, our five older brothers committed little to paper. Nevertheless, as we wrote about our own lives, especially our childhood, we wanted also to record the lives of our much-loved family. Since 1980, we have together written more than eight hundred pages of Buchele family history! What follows here is a condensation of those pages: the story of our growing up on a Kansas farm during the Great Depression, and of our five older brothers, our father, who died early, and our beloved widowed mother, who inspired us all.

Since there seems to be no limit to the Buchele clan's intelligence, ambition, industry, and accomplishments, we invite the spouses, children, and grandchildren to record their own histories and memories, and to add to ours.

Luther and Wesley Buchele

June 2008

Acknowledgments

We are much indebted to Flora Holroyd, whose 1972 "A Holroyd Genealogy" gave us the information recorded here about the Holroyd family. Before Mother Bessie died, she gave Luther family charts about the Bucheles in Ohio and the Fishers in Indiana. In September 1988, Phyllis Buchele's "Family Information Booklet" compiled the names of the grandchildren of Charles J. and Bessie Fisher Buchele. As of April 2008, the seven sons had produced twenty-three grandchildren as well as numerous great-grandchildren and great-great-grandchildren.

The Internet will no doubt be an excellent source of further information. Luther's son Royd has a family website, www.Buchele.org, that includes photographs and genealogy back to 1600; Wesley's son Steven has a blog, www.Buchele.blogspot.com, that describes his missionary family's experiences in Ghana.

In July 2007, we asked Eve Silberman, a writer for the Ann Arbor *Observer*, to read our voluminous memoirs and provide this condensation. We are grateful for her efforts and for the editorial work of Joan Buchele and Mary Matthews.

Thanks also to Michael Hough from the Ivory Photo Shop, Ann Arbor, Michigan.

Just Call Us Lucky

Introduction

In the summer of 1975, Luther and Joan Buchele, of Ann Arbor, Michigan, with their four young children, Royd, Theresa, Libbie, and Heidi, were traveling through "Tornado Alley" in Kansas, en route to Luther's boyhood home near Cedar Vale, in southeastern Kansas on the Oklahoma border. Just seven miles away, afraid that the increasingly fierce winds would tip over their Volkswagen bus, Luther pulled over to the side of the road and told his family to lie on the floor. After a few minutes, the wind and rain stopped suddenly, and the family anxiously drove on. When they reached the side road leading to the farm home, where Luther's mother still lived, they found the road completely blocked by a fallen tree.

The family then drove to the home of Luther's older brother Paul in Cedar Vale, Luther maneuvering carefully around fallen trees. Once at Paul's, they found the electrical and phone wires down. The two families spent a long night worrying about Paul and Luther's elderly mother, Bessie Mabel (Fisher) Buchele, alone in her home. Next morning, to their relief, they discovered the house untouched. But only twenty yards to the south, the tornado had destroyed the big red barn, scene of many happy childhood memories. Shaken, their mother exclaimed, "I stood on the screened porch and watched the tornado take down the barn!"

On a tour of the Buchele brothers' farms that morning, Luther and Paul, joined by their brother Julian, discovered that another of their barns and three large machine sheds also had been destroyed by the tornado. That afternoon, Julian, who was mayor of Cedar Vale, showed Luther and his family huge numbers of downed trees, blown-over house trailers, and six empty grain boxcars lying on their sides alongside the railroad tracks.

The Buchele families mourned the loss of their beloved big red barn and what it represented. During the Great Depression, as farms around them were foreclosed, their distraught owners forced to migrate, the five younger Buchele brothers and their widowed mother had managed to hold on to their two farms, Golden Acres and Spring Branch.

This was an extraordinary accomplishment, considering both the era and the Bucheles' specific plight. American farmers had been struggling for years before the stock market crash of 1929. By the mid-1920s, market prices for farm products (meats, grains, and fibers) had begun to decline, leaving the farmers stuck with surpluses. There were many reasons for the falling prices. For one, tractors were replacing horses, and the resulting efficiencies of mechanization allowed farmers to grow more commodities. But just as the grain surpluses were increasing, the horse population was falling (it declined from 27 million to 17 million between 1920 and 1929). With reduced demand for the oats and hay grown to feed horses, farmers turned to raising wheat and corn, increasing surpluses of those crops. Then, after the stock market collapsed and the Great Depression began, people without work were unable to buy food even at reduced prices, further lowering demand for the increasing surpluses. Finally, to make matters even worse, the early 1930s in Kansas were times of terrible weather conditions: drought, dust storms, floods, hail storms, and, like a biblical curse, grasshopper invasions.

In these worst of times, the five brothers still at home and their mother struggled, not only to survive, but also to pay off a $5,000 mortgage. That debt was the result of a lawsuit bitterly waged against Bessie by her brothers, Edgar and John Fisher. In brief: In 1920, Bessie and Charles Buchele had borrowed money from her father's trust fund to help them buy part of Golden Acres, which became the family farm. Pressed by her brothers six years later to repay the loan, Bessie and Charles countered that the loan should be forgiven, since Bessie had been her brothers' unpaid housekeeper for many years. Sadly, the two parties ended up in court. Luther recalls that when a lawyer came to the house to talk to his parents, he and Wesley, then six years old, were sent to the cellar, "out of the way."

The judge not only ruled against Charles and Bessie but ordered them to pay her brothers' legal fees. To raise the money, they were forced to mortgage their half-portion of Golden Acres for $5,000, at 10 percent interest. (In 2008 dollars, that mortgage debt is the equivalent of nearly $60,000.) Luther remembers "this debt hung over the heads of the Buchele brothers through the Depression as if it was a heavy rock suspended from the ceiling by a weak rope."

When Mother Bessie was widowed in 1931, neighbors advised her to give up the farm, move into town, and take in laundry. But she was determined that with her boys she would stick it out—through sweat and hard work. Three-quarters of a century later, Luther remembers the struggle. "With one IHC Farmall tractor," he recalls, "we took turns plowing, tilling, and harvesting our own fields—and sharecropping the fields of neighbors—24 hours a day, all of us taking turns running the lone tractor and sleeping."

"We had no choice," notes Wesley, a retired college professor and noted inventor of agricultural equipment. "We had to survive."

They did more than survive. Bessie Buchele wanted a better future for her sons. As they milked cows, baled hay, and plowed fields, their mother, a former schoolteacher, lectured them every day about the importance of higher education. Not all seven of the Buchele boys completed college, but all of them went, and all found success in what Luther describes as "caring" professions. He had a long career as executive secretary of the University of Michigan student cooperative housing. Wesley became a college professor. Two Buchele sons became doctors; three others were successful farmers. All the family members supported each other and shared the goal of keeping the family farm alive, and their struggles influenced their career choices.

The Linchpin:
Mother Bessie (1883–1981)

"Mother was the healthiest and most hard-working person I have ever known," Wesley writes. Bessie Fisher Buchele was born on June 12, 1883, on the Fisher ranch west of Wauneta, Kansas. As a child, she survived diphtheria and, while her family home was being built, a fall from the second floor to the basement. In college, she contracted typhoid fever. Most devastating for her, at age eleven she suffered the suicide of her mother, Mary Ann Holroyd Fisher. The hushed legends of the Fisher family are that Mary Ann, deeply depressed, and pregnant with her ninth child, hanged herself from a barn rafter. James Leonard Fisher had an epitaph chiseled on his wife's gravestone, which read in part, "Good night, loved ones, do not weep/I'm weary of earth, I long to sleep."

Mother Bessie often bragged that she "reared six families during her lifetime." Her "first family" was the one she was born into. After her mother died, an adolescent Bessie acted as "chief cook and bottle washer," caring for her four younger sisters, her two brothers, and her father. Tragically, her older sister, Anna Marila Fisher Leonard, like their mother, suffered from depression and was in and out of mental hospitals until her death in 1938. Bessie's "second family" consisted of the youngest of Anna Marila's three sons, Ernest. Along with her aunt, Ada Lewelen Holroyd, Bessie nurtured Ernest from the early 1900s until 1913. Luther writes that Ernest adored his Aunt Bessie, ultimately requesting permission to be buried in her family plot in the Ozro Falls Cemetery.

Bessie's "third family" comprised Charles John Buchele's sons from his first marriage, Robert Leroy and Charles Ned (called Ned). She had known the two little boys from teaching them in Sunday school and often said she "fell in love" with them before she even met their father.

Her "fourth family" were her husband, Charles, and the five sons born to them: James Paul (called Paul), Julian Milton, Matthew John, and the twins, Luther Holroyd and Wesley Fisher Buchele.

Bessie called Paul and Helen Fettig Buchele's children her "fifth family." She took care of James, Verona, and Kenneth while Helen helped to run the farm.

Finally, Bessie's "sixth family": Julian and Vergie Bryant Buchele's children. Bessie cared for Nancy, Carol,

Barbara, and Phyllis while Vergie, like Helen, helped on the farm. Both Vergie and Helen were also trained as bookkeepers.

In 1901, Bessie Fisher graduated in the fourth class of the new Cedar Vale High School. She later attended what was then Emporia Teachers College in Emporia, Kansas. On one frightening occasion while there, she contracted typhoid fever. She telegraphed her father, who lived on the ranch near Wauneta, and then, ill as she was, traveled the sixty-three miles to Moline by train. Her brother Ed met the train with a lumber wagon, wrapped her in blankets and laid her on a bed of hay in the bottom of the wagon, then hauled her in a driving rain twenty miles south to the family ranch.

For eleven years, Bessie Fisher taught in both county schools and at the Cedar Vale Grade School, where she was paid $80 a month. She enjoyed her freedom and her financial independence: in 1911, she took the train with a group to visit Yellowstone National Park and the West Coast. And she managed to buy Spring Branch farm near the county grade school where she was teaching.

Her life took a major turn in 1912. As Bessie recalled it, "I was teaching in the Cedar Vale Grade School near the old livery stable. I was walking to my father's home on the northeast side of town after school when a man jumped down out of the hayloft of the livery stable in front of me. He startled me. I screamed!"

Charles John Buchele apologized eloquently for frightening her. At the age of thirty-nine, he must have been attractive to a twenty-nine-year-old woman approaching spinsterhood. He was a debonair, tall, handsome, dark-haired blade with a swarthy complexion. To top it off, he had numerous gold crowns on his teeth, which flashed when he smiled. He was a good singer who belted out "The Holy City" in a lyric tenor that, Luther writes, "could make you want to weep."

Charles was in Cedar Vale to visit sons Robert and Ned, who were living with his sisters, Kate Buchele Rothrock and Sophia Buchele Aley. He and Bessie were married later that year, on November 27, 1912. It was not to be a happily-ever-after life. Bessie had to contend with her husband's unfaithfulness and bad temper. After his untimely death, she reared her boys alone while struggling to keep a farm going during the Depression. Luther recalls seeing her weeping while she washed the dishes, simply overwhelmed by the unrelenting pressures of her life. Still, toughened by her childhood and sustained by a deep religious faith, Bessie triumphed. She remained on her farm just east of Cedar Vale for almost sixty years. Writes Luther, "My mother, in my mind's eye, had the stance of the pioneer mother cast in bronze statues you see on many state capitol lawns throughout the West."

Charles John Buchele (1873–1931)

Charles Buchele was born near Liberty Center, Napoleon County, Ohio, on March 4, 1873, the youngest of the ten children of Christian Johannes Buchele and Crezenzia Singer Buchele. Strong and thrifty immigrants, Charles's parents had come to Ohio from Bavaria, Germany, in the early 1850s. They worked the farmland along the Maumee River west of Toledo to rear their large family.

After leaving home, Charles became a grain miller in Liberty Center, Ohio, and in Bluffton and Lafayette, Indiana. His business card showed his toddler son, Robert, standing in a flour bag up to his neck. The bag advertised, "Buchele Gilt Edge and Golden Wedding Flour." Family legend has it that Charles went broke in the flour milling business and afterward became a traveling salesman of household wares and "fine china." His first wife, Myrtle Ritenour, died of tuberculosis in 1909 in Liberty Center, when Robert was five and Ned three. Fortunately, Charles's sisters in Cedar Vale took them until Charles married Bessie, three years later.

Bessie had purchased Spring Branch farm, close to the rural school where she was teaching; the pristine Spring Branch Creek ran through it. She and Charles hunkered down to the daunting tasks of farming and rearing their growing family. Although their farm was five miles from town, Charles and Bessie started a raw milk delivery route, using a horse-drawn caravan. Bessie assumed the dairymaid's duty of washing milk bottles and bottling the milk. In 1919, the family bought half of Caney River farm, one and a half miles east of Cedar Vale, from Bessie's sister Grace, and moved the family there. Charles renamed it, painting "Golden Acres Farm" in large white letters on the west side of the big red barn. He then painted his name, "CHARLES J BUCHELE," underneath the farm name, as people did back in Ohio. Cedar Vale residents could read the words on the barn all the way from town. It was in this farmhouse, on March 18, 1920, that the two youngest Buchele boys, twins Luther and Wesley, were born.

The family's white saltbox house was lit at night and in early morning with coal oil lamps, Luther and Wesley remember. "A wood- fired cook range heated the kitchen and a barrel stove heated the living room." When the uphill spring flowed through a pipe into the house, or when the wind turned the windmill, there was running water. "During the calm, drought days," there was "running" water only "when someone 'ran' from the well to the house with a bucket of water."

Bessie knew about but could not control Charles's philandering. Charles left much to be desired as a father, too. Although he bragged about his handsome brood of sons, he worked them hard, displayed an evil temper, and (except for the twins, whom he apparently favored) whipped them frequently and with little provocation, using either a long stick handily stuck in the molding above the kitchen door or, later, a canvas belt.

Wesley remembers the day he, Luther, and Matthew were riding bareback on a horse. When the horse shied suddenly, Luther and Wes fell off. Father caught the horse, pulled Matthew off, and immediately whipped him with a stick. Another time, Julian forgot to shut the gate, and the cows got out. Julian was whipped. Years later, recalling the beatings, the older brothers spoke with bitterness about their father. Writes Luther, "One brother's voice box always tightened up when he talked about Charles, sounding forced and crackling as if he was confessing a great sin or crime."

Charles Buchele's death was dramatic and pitiful. One evening in 1931, when Luther and Wes were eleven years old and in the fifth grade, Charles came home ranting and raving from a farm sale near Cloverdale, seven miles north of Cedar Vale. He had purchased a needed cream separator, along with many things he didn't need at all. Much of what he was saying was gibberish. He seemed to be talking to friends who weren't there.

Wes remembers seeing his schoolmates the next day talking in huddles while staring at him. One girl broke away from the group and asked him, "What happened to your dad yesterday?" Confused, Wes replied that he didn't know. At home, Mother Bessie and the older boys spoke in hushed tones, again leaving the twins in the dark. That night, Luther and Wesley were wakened by Charles raving in a loud voice in a one-sided conversation, intermittently laughing and singing. Peeking into the downstairs bedroom, they saw that brother Robert, by then a physician, had arrived from Durant, Oklahoma. He had given their father a sedative shot, and Charles was experiencing a morphine "high."

Later, standing at the foot of their father's bed, the bewildered twins listened as Charles recounted his life history to an imaginary audience He sang and laughed; Wes wishes he could have recorded it. The next morning, Robert and Paul drove their father 200 miles to the Still-Hildreth Osteopathic Hospital in Kansas City, Missouri. As he was taken from the farm, he sang to Bessie, "Let me call you sweetheart." Charles was eventually transferred to the Osawatomie Sanatorium for the Insane in Kansas.

Wes remembers his mother mailing his father a homemade cake for his fifty-eighth birthday on March 4, 1931. Two months later, on May 15, Charles Buchele, the handsome, irresponsible, dark-tempered man, died of a disease commonly called "brain fever" but actually diagnosed as syphilis. Wes recalls weeping in the back seat of the Model-T Ford on the way to the funeral. Much less distraught, Luther remembers pretending to stumble down the church steps, as though in grief. But most of the Bucheles were dry-eyed, more angry than grief-stricken. In that era, the terrible stigma of the disease disgraced the family. Mother Bessie and the brothers had blood drawn and were tested for syphilis; happily, they all tested negative.

Charles Buchele rests in the Buchele plot of the Ozro Falls Cemetery southeast of Cedar Vale. Bessie lived another fifty years, to the age of ninety-eight. She was buried alongside Charles.

Robert Leroy (1904–1986)

Robert Leroy, sometimes "Bob" and later sometimes "Doc," the eldest of the seven Buchele boys, was born on April 26, 1904, at Liberty Center, Ohio. His birth mother died in 1909, when he was five and Ned was three; Bessie became their stepmother three years later. Mother Bessie always boasted that she considered Robert and Ned her "own boys," making no distinction between them and her biological children, never treating them differently.

The responsibilities of being the eldest weighed heavily on Robert's shoulders. He was hard to please. As kids, Luther and Wes called him "Grouch." Because he was fifteen years older than they were, they remember little about his years at home before he went off to Southwestern College in Winfield, Kansas, in 1922. A year later, Robert enrolled in the Kansas City Osteopathic College in Kansas City, Missouri, and in 1926 began practicing osteopathic medicine in Durant, Oklahoma. Luther and Wesley recall that he shipped a gunnysack full of raw peanuts from Durant to the family in Cedar Vale each Christmas.

After four years in Durant, contending with loneliness and a low income, Bob moved to Howard, Kansas, the county seat of Elk County, about thirty-five miles northeast of Cedar Vale. He practiced there for over fifty years.

In 1939, Robert married Irma Marian McCollough, a high school mathematics teacher. For many years, Irma was her husband's factotum—office manager, accountant, and practical nurse. Childless, the couple rented a cramped upstairs apartment in a house near their office. When their landlady died, in the 1980s, they bought it and it became their lifelong home. For many years, Dr. Robert was the only doctor in all of Elk County; during his practice he delivered 150 babies.

Bob visited the Buchele family about once a month, walking the fields with his younger half-brothers and offering advice. He was the only Santa Claus the children ever knew. When he visited at Christmas, he brought thick socks and mittens, which not only kept their feet and hands warm in the winter but also made them feel more kindly toward their big doctor-brother. He also treated their illnesses, particularly Paul's back problems.

A Republican, Robert was elected to the Kansas State House of Representatives in 1948 and stayed for almost a decade. His major achievement was a bill that permitted osteopathic doctors to write prescriptions, a privilege previously enjoyed only by medical doctors. All fifty states have since enacted similar laws. Also, listening to his inner farmer, Dr. Bob raised hogs on a farm Irma had inherited.

Sadly, tensions developed between Robert and Irma, staunch Republicans, and his stepbrother Paul's son Jim, who, nine years after Robert left the state legislature, was elected from another district to the Kansas State House of Representatives, but as a Democrat. Robert and Irma's visits to Cedar Vale became less frequent, and when they did come, Irma remained in the car. Unhappily, the estrangement continued throughout Dr. Robert's lifetime. In retrospect, Luther expresses a "sneaking suspicion" that Mother Bessie and daughter-in-law Irma clashed over Bessie's "motherly advice" not to take political affiliation too seriously. Yet, though Bessie and Irma stopped speaking, Irma remained on friendly terms with Robert's brothers and their families, who continued to visit her after his death. Luther recalls that Irma didn't seem disturbed by his own socialist leanings and that she responded promptly to his letters until her death in 2006.

In the late 1970s, Dr. Robert gave $50,000 to the town of Howard, Kansas, to build a community center, and it was named for him. The village honored him with a dedication ceremony on "Dr. Robert Buchele Day," attended by his mother and his brothers and their families. He died at age eighty-two, in 1991; Irma died fifteen years later on February 24, 2006. Robert and Irma are buried in the Howard, Kansas, Memorial Cemetery.

Charles Ned (1906–2000)

Wes believes that Ned was probably "one of the last true gentlemen in the world." To his dying day, Ned tipped his hat to ladies as he passed them on the street and always took his hat off when he came into the house. Ned was even-tempered and mild-mannered, more outgoing than the somewhat dour Robert. "Everyone liked him," says Luther. The twins even forgave him for killing Santa Claus. Eager four-year-olds, they had hung their long stockings on the bookcase behind the round wood stove, only to find next morning that Ned had filled them with corncobs and peanut shells!

In 1923, after high school, Ned enrolled in the Agronomy Department of Kansas State Agricultural College, in Manhattan, Kansas. Though he attended for just one year, he learned a lot about farming. He returned home and worked on the family farm for a time. Later, he clerked at the Cedar Vale Co-op Store, where he met his future wife, Thelma Grace Noland, whose mother was his boss. The couple was married on February 15, 1929, and after a honeymoon trip in a black Model-T Ford coupe with a rumble seat, they began farming Spring Branch farm, two miles east of Golden Acres. It was the first of five farmsteads Ned was to sharecrop during his life. Thelma, a city girl, enjoyed the "IcyBall," an early gasoline-fired Electrolux refrigerator that sat on the front porch of their red stone house.

An astute farmer, Ned worried about the carbon-nitrogen ratio of the soil and how the date of plowing under oat stubble affected that ratio and the corn crop. As a result, he practiced crop rotation even before 1935, the year that the "fathers of soil conservation," Franklin Roosevelt's secretary of agriculture, Henry Wallace, and Hugh Bennett, established what became the federal Soil Conservation Service. The government began paying farmers to rotate their crops, terrace their fields, and build ponds.

As his half-brothers grew to maturity Ned began farming on his own, mortgaging his cattle to buy supplies and equipment. By 1932, corn was selling for twelve cents a bushel and hogs for seven cents a pound. A quart of milk wholesaled for four cents and retailed for five cents. One day, Ed Bradley, vice-president of the Cedar Vale National Bank, said to Ned, "I sure am worried about our cattle." Ned replied, "Well, if you are going to worry about my cattle, I won't. There's no need for both of us worrying about them!"

Ned and Thelma's children, sons Keith and Marvin, exchanged farm work with Ned's younger brothers, Paul and Julian, who farmed as partners for more than fifty-four years. Thelma died in 1956. Ten years later, Ned married Ina Oliver Julian, who clerked in Woolworth's Five and Ten Cent Store in Moline. Ned farmed together with his younger son, Marvin, until he retired in 1974. Ina died in 1998 and is buried in Lawrence, Kansas. Ned died on December 5, 2000, at the age of ninety-four, at St. John's Regional Medical Center in Joplin, Missouri, where his grandson Alan Buchele was a surgeon. Thelma and Ned rest in the Moline, Kansas, Memorial Cemetery.

James Paul (1913–1992),
the First of the "Great Brothers"

Luther and Wesley, out of respect, love, and admiration, refer to Paul and Julian as the "great brothers."

After their father died, the twins recall, Paul "was our father." But, writes Luther, "I doubt Paul knew he was playing a father role." After all, Paul was only seven years older than they were. Still, "Mother told us that when Dad's estate was probated that the judge in a dramatic moment said to Mother and to eighteen-year-old Paul, a senior in high school, 'Mother, behold thy son. Son, behold thy mother.'"

Paul frequently acted as the family decision-maker. In 1931 a man named John Ott, the unemployed father of three, approached the brothers seeking a job. "How much pay do you need?" Paul asked. When Ott replied, "Oh, about a dollar" (the equivalent of $12.31 in 2008), Paul reflected and then said, "I think a dollar an hour is too much to pay for farm work." Mr. Ott hastily answered, "No, I wasn't asking for a dollar an hour—I meant a dollar a day." Paul hired him, warmly telling him, "Please don't carry a lunch tomorrow. We welcome you to have dinner with our family."

A convert to osteopathic treatments, Paul "rubbed all our pains and hurts away," recall the twins. He was also midwife when mother cows experienced difficult births. Poignantly, despite his caring abilities, Paul himself often needed special care. He had suffered since childhood from a rapid heartbeat and high blood pressure. At twelve, he broke his right elbow falling from a tree while picking wild grapes. In his later years, he suffered from a torn retina, and each of his worn-out hip joints had to be replaced.

Luther and Wesley remember that because Paul seemed so much older than they were, he was fifteen or sixteen "before we paid much attention to him. But he was there in the shadows while we all herded the milk cows into the big red barn, pitched hay into the mangers below, fed the cats with a milk stream from the cow's teat, cleaned the chicken houses, gathered eggs, slopped the pigs, plowed the field behind a team of horses, and shocked oats and wheat."

Paul was the only Buchele boy to become a Boy Scout, and the other brothers reveled in his scout paraphernalia—his strange-smelling uniform and the knife, knife-holder, whetstone, telescope, backpack, large-brimmed khaki hat, and *Scout Handbook*. The handbook gave instruction in everything from cooking over a campfire to using Morse code. Best of all, Paul received monthly issues of *Boys' Life*, which the younger boys devoured. They loved looking at the pictures of scouts saluting the flag and hiking, and reading the scary adventure stories of their tents being invaded by fierce bears.

More than the other brothers, Paul was a "read-a-holic." The twins, unsympathetic to Paul's frequently having his "nose in a book," nagged him, sometimes even trying to snatch his book away. But Paul always held on. Although his brothers complained that he should be working, not reading, it would be Paul, along with Julian, who took over the family farms. Theirs was a very successful lifelong partnership. Julian was the dreamer, musing over what might be and sometimes stumbling; Paul was the more steady, likely to offer reasoned resistance to his brother's visions. Paul was the mechanical inventor and guardian of the tools and equipment, knowing where all the junk parts and tools were kept. Julian had a better memory for livestock, knowing how many cattle were in each pasture and apparently even remembering each cow, steer, or calf by its markings. He knew each animal's dam and sire and where it had been purchased. "Considering that they might have had up to 500 animals," Luther writes, "I found his memory phenomenal!"

Paul married Helen Fettig, a onetime hired girl for the family, in 1940, and together they reared three children, James, Verona, and Kenneth. Like her husband, Helen was a natural caretaker. They cared for Bessie Buchele, for Helen's parents in their old age, and for Julian in his later years. While a student at the University of Kansas (KU), Luther stayed with Paul and Helen during vacations and helped them farm, frequently becoming ill, perhaps from Paul and Helen's kids' childhood ailments. "What a pain in the neck I must have been," Luther remarked in a tribute at Paul and Helen's fiftieth wedding anniversary.

Paul was active in his community and in the Baptist Church, where he sang in the choir. He spent long, probably frustrating, years on various boards of directors: of the Cedar Vale Cooperative, the Co-op Exchange, the Cedar Vale Cooperative Elevator, and the Rural Electrification Administration. He served on the board of directors of the Kansas State Board of Agriculture for seventeen years, several of them as president, and on the Board of State Fair Managers, a job he especially enjoyed. Paul died on March 17, 1992, at age seventy-nine, and Helen on February 6, 2008. Both are buried in the Ozro Falls Cemetery family plot.

Julian Milton (1915–1983), the Second "Great Brother"

O ne of Luther's first memories of Julian is of the time Julian broke his arm. He and Wesley were about ten and Julian sixteen when the three of them, leaving the supper dishes unwashed, ran up the hill with Paul and Matthew to the large red barn Grandfather Fisher had built. On the north side of the barn they kept a thick hay-stacker rope to use for playing jump rope. Julian was jumping while Matthew and Paul turned the rope. He stumbled, falling forward and hitting the ground that sloped toward the barn. Instinctively, he put out his arm, breaking it as he fell. While their mother and Paul took Julian to the doctor to have his arm set, the chagrined Matthew and the twins went back home "with our tails limp behind us," says Luther, and "without being told, did the dishes."

Possibly the handsomest of a clan of good-looking boys, Julian was also strong as an ox and rarely saw a doctor. (Only at the end of his life was he frail, after he developed diabetes and suffered a stroke.) Julian was a high school football hero. After a Thanksgiving game with Moline High, the most competitive team in the league, the family discovered that Julian had been "sort of knocked out," but had continued to play—without even realizing he'd been injured! The story of Julian's unintentional bravery was told so often the twins got sick of it. They were proud of Julian's success, but it also rankled, because when Julian—and later Matthew—stayed after school for football practice, it was the twins who had to hurry home and start the farm chores: bringing in the cows from the pasture and milking them, slopping the hogs, gathering the eggs, feeding the chickens— "ad nauseum," Luther writes.

Later, Wesley also played high school football. Luther, who was clumsy in sports, was jealous. He developed what he describes as a "lifelong hatred and contempt for all team competitive sports."

After high school, Julian completed two semesters at KU. He dreamed of playing football, only to discover that he was a runt compared to the bruisers on the team. He wanted to be a civil engineer, but found the math too much for him, and anyway he worried constantly about the farm. So he finally threw in the towel and returned home.

Like Paul, Julian could be a calming influence on the twins—particularly on Luther, who admits to having his father's bad temper. One morning in August 1940, the family was discussing Paul's upcoming wedding; Luther, twenty, found himself becoming agitated. "It might have been related to my suspicion that I would have to run the dairy almost single-handedly for the two weeks of their honeymoon," he remembers. "I made a caustic remark about the situation, and Mother said that I was a 'bad boy.' I responded by tossing my cup of coffee at her in anger. I can still see the cream-colored coffee filming Mother's glasses and dripping from her face." (Fortunately, the coffee was tepid.) Julian hit Luther on the arm and took him outside. Writes Luther: "I always appreciated Julian's restraint in being the kindly but firm father."

Several years after that, Luther noticed that Julian was spending a lot of time shopping at the Bryant Hardware store in nearby Arkansas City, Kansas. He finally learned that Julian was courting Vergie Bryant, the owner's daughter and a clerk at the store. She had just returned from service in World War II as a member of the WASPs (Women's Airforce Service Pilots). Vergie and Julian were married on November 26, 1947, and became the parents of four daughters, Nancy, Carol, Barbara, and Phyllis.

Julian and Paul continued their farming partnership in Cedar Vale, and despite the hazards of farming, were blessed with success. Julian and Vergie had been married for thirty-six years when she died in her sleep, in 1983, of complications from diabetes and heart disease. Julian never fully recovered from his loss, though his four daughters provided much care and comfort. He died on September 11, 1987, at age seventy-two. Julian and Vergie are buried in the Buchele family plot in the Ozro Falls Cemetery.

Matthew John (1917–1983)

Despite the backbreaking work, difficult weather, and (by today's standards) primitive farm machinery, all of the brothers took naturally to farm work—except Matthew, "born *not* to be a farm boy," Luther observes. Around the time Matthew was graduating from high school, Wesley and Luther, snooping through the clothes closet off the second-floor bedroom they shared with Matthew, discovered a small cache of money under a rug. They "gleefully" displayed "the fortune" to the family. Matthew soon confessed to having salted away some of the money collected from the dairy route in hopes of financing study at KU.

Because their mother had for so long stressed the importance of higher education, no one held his money-saving against Matthew. In fact, the family decided it was time for both him and Paul to go to college. To economize, they would share an apartment.

These were exciting times for the family! On the day of their older brothers' departure, Luther and Wesley were sitting in their typing class at school, near a large window overlooking the highway. They paused to watch their old black panel truck traveling down the highway, laden with furniture, bedding, dishes, cooking utensils, and foodstuffs. Paul and Matthew had gassed up the truck at the Co-op Exchange service station and were headed 200 miles north to Lawrence and the University of Kansas!

Matthew deserved the break. He was unfortunately positioned in the household. There is a family story that Matthew, with two older brothers and just two-and-a-half years old when the twins were born, declared to his mother with shock, "Two babies, Mother, *two* babies!" Matthew quickly realized that the twins—whom he named "Lute" and "Hest"—had displaced him as the baby of the family and, moreover, that the cute little guys were out to make his life miserable. Recalls Luther, "Because he was our older brother, he tried to lord it over us twins, and to get even we plotted mischief. We taunted him, we wouldn't play with him, we ran away from him, and we pestered him to death!"

As a teenager, Matthew developed a massive case of acne, which scarred his face for life. Luther says, "We contrived to give him a new nickname. It wasn't as if he didn't have a horrible one already: the family called him 'Snick'—for what reasons I have no idea. With his afflictions [Matthew wet his bed for years], we thought up a new nickname, 'Pee-Bed—Pimples.' In public, we called him "PBP."

Matthew was probably happier in school, where he excelled in arithmetic and won several Chautauqua County grade school math contests. His prizes, along with several framed paintings, still hang in the Cedar Vale Grade School. "He certainly was not happy working on the farm—even the horses seemed to know it and dislike him," Wesley writes. "Once, a large, matched team of black Percheron horses, Dick and Sam, backed away from their manger and began to kick him. Matthew returned to the house battered and bruised," Wesley recalls, with "an even deeper hatred for horses and farming." On another occasion, while cultivating corn, Matthew was heard shouting at the top of his voice, "I hate farming!"

While at KU, Matthew met his future wife, Adelma Watson, who, like him, graduated with a BS degree in bacteriology. The two were married shortly after graduation, on August 23, 1941. Once the United States entered the war, Matthew served in New Guinea for three years, in the Sanitary Corps of the U.S. Army Air Corps. During that time, Adelma lived in Detroit and drove a truck for the Army. When the war ended, Matthew went through Baylor University Medical School and then set up practice in San

Augustine, Texas. He and Adelma reared four children: Michael, Barry, Carolyn, and Craig. In addition to her responsibilities as wife and mother, Adelma was Dr. Matthew's office factotum, just as Irma was Dr. Robert's.

Interestingly, the couple brought their children to the family farms in Kansas during vacations, and Matthew—he who had screamed, "I hate farming!"—would work alongside them, believing, reflects Luther, that the hard work built character. Matthew died on July 8, 1983, at sixty-six, of stomach cancer and complications of diabetes. The St. Augustine Hospital named its new wing the Matthew J. Buchele Wing, and the local Lions Club later installed a memorial chapel there to honor him and the care he had given the people of East Texas. Adelma lived for another twenty-four years and died in Austin on February 5, 2007. She and Matthew are interred in the San Augustine Cemetery.

The Twins:
Luther Holroyd and Wesley Fisher (1920–)

For many years, Wesley and Luther (age eighty-eight in March of 2008) committed to paper their memories of what they consider, despite all its hardships and even heartbreak, a happy childhood. One reason for its happiness was their special bond as twins. They write: "Luther, the sixth son, says Wes was creative and adventuresome. Wes, the seventh son, says Luther was a most kind and thoughtful twin brother." Although as adults they differed in the potentially explosive areas of politics and religion, both say they have never quarreled. They were so close, says Luther, that after he married, at age forty, he was surprised that his wife, Joan, unlike Wes, could not immediately anticipate his thoughts.

Until they went to college, Luther to the University of Kansas, Wes to Kansas State Agricultural College, the twins were inseparable. They didn't look alike, but neighbors still had trouble telling them apart and referred to them simply as "the twins." As "built-in" company for each other, they entertained themselves uniquely, and at an early age—four or five—they began to "tick," as they called it, developing and discussing imaginary characters and inventing their accomplishments. At first, their playmates were "babies," Luther recalls, who "owned fabulous estates, were champions of the poor, and stalwart in matters of civic duty and ethical behavior."

This playful, competitive "ticking" continued until the twins were ten or eleven. "Our babies" became "our bears," Luther remembers. "Part of the stories were pure bravado—my bear would do this (and in my mind he had done it), and Wesley would top the exploit, telling of *his* bear's performance." Luther would say, "My bear won the county spelling contest, and in his honor his third grade classroom was given a picture of 'The Gleaners,' by Millet." Wesley would retort, "My bear won the 100-yard dash race at the county sports meet, and to honor him, his classroom was given a softball bat!"

As they grew older, the twins began to grasp the enormity of the Depression and to understand that others were suffering even more than the Buchele family. Luther will never forget the time in 1925 when his father took the five-year-old twins to a farm bankruptcy auction and, to their delight, bought them a "goat cart" with red side boards. After the sale, when the twins went to claim their cart, they found the farmer's sons playing with it. Wesley grabbed the tongue of the cart from one of the boys and started pulling it away; the farmer's boys moved to the back of the cart and grabbed the end board. Luther, of course, helped Wesley. "It was a pulling match, which even today at the age of eighty-seven stresses my gut," Luther writes. "In my mind's eye the pathos of the picture symbolizes the struggle between the haves and the have-nots. I'm sure that for the first time in my life I felt the situational pain of poor people that may have helped to move me to my career choice to work for cooperatives and become a socialist."

Their different interests took shape as the twins grew up. Wesley's mechanical mind and ability to make things with his hands grew stronger, and he began spending a lot of time in the workshop. There was a constant supply of old lumber, plaster lathe, and farm implements around to use in imaginative ways. Wes made a toy disc plow of lathe, wire, and Mason jar lids, and a life-like hay baler that actually worked.

For his part, Luther read more than his twin, and also developed cooking, decorating, and organizing skills. He was embarrassed, he recalls, when his mother once told the ladies at church that he had baked the cake for the church dinner.

These were early signs of the skills the twins would draw on in their very different, very successful careers.

Luther and Wes followed their brothers' example, working long and hard hours on the farm. And for one exhausting year, 1935–1936, when they were just fifteen, the burden of keeping the farm going fell almost entirely on them. Matthew and Julian were in college, and Paul was in bed for a year, recovering from heart problems. In addition to routine farm work, the twins made the daily dairy deliveries, despite their embarrassment at having their classmates see them delivering the bottled milk.

When Luther and Paul both fell ill with scarlet fever and were quarantined, Wes and the hired man, Harold Snodgrass, had to do all the work. On one occasion, Wes, by then of driving age, was so exhausted that he fell asleep during the milk deliveries and bumped into another car. Fortunately, the worst damage was to his ego!

Somehow, despite the never-ending demands of the farm, Wes and Luther enjoyed outside interests, particularly the Spring Branch 4-H Club, where they became leaders. In 1938, at eighteen, they were chosen the "most outstanding" 4-H boys in the state of Kansas. "This is the first time in my recollection that this award has gone to two boys jointly," marveled the 4-H official in the letter announcing their award.

While in 4-H, the twins wrote and presented two demonstrations: "How To Make Capons" and "How To Produce Clean Milk." They were more than a little nervous about delivering "How To Make Capons," since removal of a rooster's testicles was a delicate topic. The Buchele family always roared with laughter about one demonstration, on Labor Day 1937, at the Cedar Vale Park pavilion. Everything was going fine until Luther began to remove the rooster's second testicle. Somehow he cut a blood vessel, and the rooster died on the spot. The script called for him to remove the bird from the holding device, set it on its feet, and declare enthusiastically, "The operation hasn't hurt him a bit!" Luther held the dead rooster by his wings, flapped them up and down, and shouted, "See how lively he is! The operation hasn't hurt him a bit!" He immediately tossed the dead bird into the coop behind the demonstration table, and he and Wes hurried off the stage.

The twins were helped in their capon demonstration by George Bowie, the nation's only manufacturer of caponizing tools, who was a Cedar Vale resident to whom the boys delivered milk. He gave them a set of the tools and wrote a very complimentary article about them. In it, Bowie asserted that Luther and Wesley had saved their mother's mortgaged farm from foreclosure by raising and selling capons. He sent the article, along with photographs of the demonstration, to several poultry magazines. After the story appeared, Luther recalls, "Wesley and I soon began receiving fan-mail letters telling us what good boys we were to help our poor old widowed mother!" The article failed to mention that the twins had raised only one capon to maturity!

Wesley was awarded a 4-H scholarship to Kansas State Agricultural College, where he earned a degree in agricultural engineering. "We didn't see much of Wesley on the farm after that," Luther remembers, "because he had joined the Kansas State ROTC program and spent one summer, in 1940, at an ROTC camp, and another summer working for the John Deere Tractor Works." Wes received his degree in 1943.

Wes spent much of World War II on bases in the United States. He married his 4-H Club friend and college sweetheart, Mary Jagger, on June 12, 1945, shortly before the war in Europe ended. Two months later, he was sent overseas as a first lieutenant. (Luther had been classified 4-F because of a hearing problem, elevated blood pressure, and color blindness.) Before he left, Wes hitched a ride to Lawrence, Kansas, to say good-bye to Luther. Luther gave him his portable pink Emerson radio, which Wes carried with him until it was destroyed in a fire at his barracks in Sapporo, Hokkaido, Japan, in 1946.

After Japan surrendered, on August 10, 1945, Wes was sent to join the occupation forces. On the ship headed for the Philippines en route to Japan, he was lying on deck reading a book when anti-aircraft guns began shooting at targets being towed by an airplane. Wes's ears received the full impact of the blast, which permanently impaired his hearing.

In September 1945, Wes found himself a platoon leader in the 81st Ordnance Company of the 81st Division, in Hirosaki, Japan. There, the Japanese captain insisted on a surrender ceremony, in which he bowed and presented Wes with his sword. To Wes, that ceremony made the earlier Japanese surrender to General Douglas MacArthur on the battleship Missouri look like a tea party. Wes was made commander of the 77th Heavy Ammunition Company until 1946, when he was placed on inactive duty and sent home. He remained in the Reserves till 1970, retiring as a major.

In September 1946, back from the war, Wes went to work again for the John Deere Tractor Works in Waterloo, Iowa. "You can take the boy off the farm, but you can't take the farm out of the boy," he jokes. In 1951 he received a master's degree in agricultural engineering from the University of Arkansas in Fayetteville, where he researched a procedure to harvest cotton mechanically, at night, more cleanly and with less waste.

Wes received his PhD, in agricultural engineering and soil physics, from Iowa State University (ISU) in Ames, for his work on ridge tillage of corn and on the helical-flow threshing cylinder, for which he received a patent. He spent most of the rest of his career as a professor there (1963–1989). He developed many courses at ISU, including one on agricultural safety, the very first college credit course of its kind in the United States.

Improving the safety and effectiveness of farm equipment has been Wes's lifelong passion. He is best known as a co-inventor of the large round-bale hay baler, now used around the world. He also helped to develop the Ridge-Till sustainable farming system to prevent soil erosion. Always eager to reduce machine-related farm accidents, Wes testifies frequently on behalf of victims, Luther proudly points out.

Beyond his wartime service overseas in the Philippines and Japan, Wes taught and conducted research in a number of countries during his career. He worked for the Agricultural Research Service of the U.S. Department of Agriculture, the State Department, and in the United States

Agency for International Development (USAID) of the U.S. Department of State.

In 1968–1969, he and his family spent a memorable year in Ghana while he taught agricultural mechanization at the University of Ghana. He describes his mission there, and in all the underdeveloped countries he went to, as going "beyond teaching to promoting the development of manufacturing industries by the village blacksmiths, using the United States as a model. Until the mid-1940s, every village in the U.S.A. had a blacksmith shop, because horses powered the American farm, and farmers needed to shoe their horses frequently. Blacksmiths became the captains of industry, like Cyrus McCormick, John Deere, and James Oliver."

In his work overseas, Wes encouraged the USAID to make small grants to local blacksmiths, "to help them buy charcoal and steel for the fabrication of such tools as spades, hoes, plows, trailers, and planters" for sale to the farmers. No grants were made, but his recommendation is "still on the books," Wes notes. In general, Wes was "disheartened by the slow progress toward development beyond the city limits" in the countries he was sent to. He taught short courses about agricultural tools to farmers in Kenya, Peru, Zambia, Tanzania, and the Philippines.

Later, in 1983, teaching agricultural mechanization in China for six months, he found that the Chinese farm machinery industry had manufactured tens of thousands of helical-flow threshing cylinders for the country's rice farmers. This was the machine Wes had invented at ISU in 1952!

Not only has Wes been granted twenty-three patents for his innovative work to improve farm machinery, but he also has been widely recognized and honored throughout his long career. He was cited for excellence in teaching by the ISU Alumni Association in 1986, and as "outstanding and eminent" by the Iowa Engineering Society in 1989. In 1988 he was honored by the American Society of Agricultural Engineers with the Cyrus Hall McCormick Jerome Increase Case Gold Medal, and in 2005 he received a Distinguished Alumni Award from the University of Arkansas College of Engineering.

Although long retired, Wes continues to lecture, and he spends ten hours every day writing about the subject he most enjoys: the history of farm machinery. He never misses a service at the Collegiate United Methodist Church in Ames, and he meets regularly with former colleagues. Happily married for fifty-five years, Wes and Mary reared two daughters, Marybeth and Sheron, and two sons, Rod and

Steve. Mary died on April 1, 2000, and is interred at the Iowa State University Cemetery in Ames.

In the late 1980s, Wes wrote a brief autobiographical essay that began, "Just call me lucky! I was born in the right place at the right time (1920) in a country of unlimited opportunities (U.S.A.)." Luther counters that he was being modest: his own drive, determination, and genius for inventing helped to create that luck.

Luther's career went in a different direction from his twin's. His life has been consistently influenced by his political convictions. During his freshman year at the University of Kansas, he met a graduate student, the socialist son of an out-of-work socialist and union organizer. Inspired by their stories, Luther embraced socialism. (Wesley voted mostly for Republicans, though he left the party out of unhappiness about the Iraq war, remarking dryly, "If George W. Bush did nothing else, he made me a Democrat.")

While Wesley remains a matter-of-fact Methodist, Luther, to his religious mother's dismay, turned away from organized religion in college. His skepticism about a Supreme Being made him feel at home among fellow doubters in the liberal Unitarian Church in Lawrence, Kansas, and since 1951 he has been active in the equally liberal First Unitarian Universalist congregation in Ann Arbor.

Luther began college a year late. When he and Wesley graduated from high school in the spring of 1938, Matthew was in his junior year at KU, and Wesley had his 4-H scholarship for the fall at Kansas State in Manhattan, Kansas. To ease the drain on the family finances, Luther opted to remain on the farm for another year. In June 1939, Luther and his mother attended Matthew's graduation ceremony. While they were in Lawrence, Luther took a lease on Matthew's room on Tennessee Street for the coming fall term and arranged to take over Matthew's delivery route of the student newspaper, *The Daily Kansan*. Matthew gave Luther his old bicycle, and one of Luther's most difficult tasks that fall was to learn how to ride a vehicle he had never ridden.

Wesley frequently hitched a ride from Manhattan to Lawrence (about eighty miles) to visit Luther, who by then was living at the Jayhawk Cooperative house. As soon as his fellow co-opers learned that Wes was from the "cow college," they serenaded him with a song, to the tune of "How Dry I Am," whose only words were "Alfalfa hay, alfalfa hay," sung ten times, with feeling!

Of course, living at the Jayhawk Co-op influenced Luther's unusual and quixotic career choice as a lifelong co-oper. But also, he emphasizes, "I have cooperatives in my genes!" His family had belonged to several co-ops: for gasoline, processing cheese and butter, hog and cattle marketing, and even grain-elevator storage. Loyal co-oper Luther recalls, though, that the farm co-op meetings he attended with his father as a child were often "long and boring."

After several years as an undergraduate, Luther chose to major in zoology. Asked why, he replies, "Unlike Wesley, I had never in my life thought much about an adult career. Since I was following brother Matthew at KU, I chose zoology." Reflecting further, he explains, "During my first four years at KU, I 'drifted' through such subjects as psychology, accounting, bacteriology, and economics, which had little to do with zoology! I think that I believed that I would eventually 'bump into' a career choice I liked, which is exactly what happened—working for cooperatives!"

After his seventh year as an undergrad, Luther was called in to the dean's office and told sternly, "You are a drain on the university's financial resources—you must graduate during the 1945 commencement!" So Luther finally received his BA degree, in zoology. He also became a proselytizer, telling undecided students, "Don't worry about declaring a major study. Take subjects that appeal to you, and eventually you'll bump into something you can happily work at the rest of your life!"

Luther started work immediately on a master's degree in biology and was hired as an instructor in the bacteriology and virology laboratories at KU for one year. For the next two years, after an FBI loyalty check, he worked in the Bacteriological Warfare Laboratory headed by his major professor, Dr. Cora Downs. Under contract to Fort Detrick in Frederick, Maryland, the KU laboratory conducted highly classified research on efficient methods of spreading *Bacterium tularense* among enemy troops. Tularemia, also called "rabbit fever," is a disease contracted while skinning infected rabbits. The bacterium is so small that it can penetrate the unbroken skin to cause a debilitating month-long illness. Inhaled into the lungs, the germs cause certain death.

While conducting the research, Luther actually became infected with the disease. A lesion formed on his left ring finger, and he was sick for a month. The research thesis for his master's degree was based on his attempts to immunize rats against Tularemia infection. One good thing to come out of Dr. Downs's laboratory research was a vaccine to immunize hunters against the dangerous infection. After he received his master's in bacteriology in 1948, Luther worked for another two years in Dr. Downs's lab.

Luther respected Dr. Downs very much, but he disliked the "wooden" individuals he worked with, who "appeared indifferent to the possible consequences of the horrible work" in biological warfare that engaged them. By the time he left, happily, in 1950, he was already deeply involved in the cooperative movement.

During his time at KU, Luther helped to organize the Central League of Campus Co-ops, in 1943, and the North American Student Cooperative League (NASCL), in 1947. He became NASCL's executive secretary in 1949, and in September 1951, he was hired as executive secretary of the Inter-Cooperative Council (ICC) at the University of Michigan.

Before he moved to Ann Arbor to begin his work with the ICC, Luther spent a memorable "vagabond" summer in Europe. He enjoyed ten days' worth of free food and lodging, courtesy of an Austrian Tourist Bureau offer to students, and later attended the International Conference of Young Cooperators in Dobriach, in southeastern Austria. He not only learned a lot about cooperative movements in Europe, but he also made friends with many attendees, afterward visiting some in their native countries.

When Mother Bessie learned of Luther's travel plans, she sent him addresses of the Buchele-Singer relatives living near Stuttgart, Germany. To him, this was to be the most important part of the trip. While visiting cousins from both sides of his father's family, he was "bitten" by the "genealogy bug," which caused a lasting infection. Genealogy has been his hobby ever since, and he has records of his antecedents dating back to the 1600s!

Several years later, in 1958, Luther attended another overseas conference, this one in Madras, India, on "Cooperative and Self-Help Techniques in the University Community." It was organized by the World University Service (WUS), which offered aid to students in Europe after World War II, and hoped to expand to underdeveloped countries. Sixty delegates representing seven countries attended the conference. The WUS leadership hoped to promote self-help projects—such as the student-run bookstores and housing co-ops popular on American campuses—as a way to reduce the cost of higher education. In a housing co-op house each member is obliged to work five or six hours a week at such household tasks as cooking or cleaning, to join in managing the house by attending house meetings, to accept an office if elected, and to share equally in the expense of running the co-op.

WUS's idealism came up against the student delegates' revulsion at the very idea of sweeping their own floors, cleaning their own bathrooms, or doing their own cooking. Working in a co-op bookstore or publishing their own course books did appeal to them, however.

Luther's report on the conference was sixteen pages; he felt his contribution was to emphasize the practical aspects of operating student cooperatives, a needed first step toward fulfilling the idealistic aims of the movement's leadership.

When Luther became executive secretary of the ICC, there were just five student co-ops in Ann Arbor. During his thirty-four years in the office, that number rose to twenty-three, and co-op membership grew from 170 students to more than 500. To Luther, the co-ops, like the Statue of Liberty, embodied tolerance, inclusiveness, and democracy. While sororities, fraternities, and the landlords of houses and apartments discriminated against African-Americans and Jews, the co-ops were open to all. Moreover, they were a great boon to needy students, who could reduce their rent and food bills by almost 30 percent by working six hours at household or management chores.

When Luther arrived in Ann Arbor in 1951, he found himself in the middle of a messy battle involving the five co-ops, their neighbors, the University of Michigan (U-M), its dean of women, and building inspectors from both the city and the university. The problems included the co-ops' untidy kitchens and yards, their late parties and loud music, their members' unpaid house bills, and after-hours visitations by members of the opposite sex. It took some sorting out! Luther had to defend the co-ops from the very particular dean of women, Deborah Bacon, whose complaints included their "untidiness." During one dispute, Luther countered, "In comparison to women in sororities, women in co-ops have cleaner minds—they don't discriminate against Blacks and Jews!"

The co-ops attracted spirited women who chafed at the curfews imposed on female students of that era. One time, the Osterweil Co-Op held an unregistered party with lots of spiked punch and loud music. When one of the girls wandered drunk onto the streets of Ann Arbor at 3 a.m., the police called the assistant dean of women, Elizabeth Leslie. Leslie called the house and was assured by the young graduate student house director that "the girls were all in."

"You are lying!" replied the infuriated assistant dean. Early the next morning, she summoned Luther, the ICC student president, the house officers, and the university building inspectors. The result: the house director was fired, and the house, under threat of closure, was forced to do a massive cleanup of the alleged "unsanitary conditions."

Not surprisingly, many activists in the national civil rights, antiwar, and women's movements of the late 1960s and early 1970s emerged from student co-ops. Luther loved being part of the sound and the fury, as the U-M campus, like those of universities around the country, erupted in protests. He even played a "modest role" in the organization of Students for a Democratic Society (SDS), the radical group whose name became synonymous with campus activism. While still unmarried, Luther often flew to New York City for meetings of the Young Adult Council. There he became friends with a woman representing the Student League for Industrial Democracy (SLID). On his invitation, she came to Ann Arbor to meet local activists, including Al Haber, the son of liberal U-M dean William Haber. Ultimately, Al Haber and two other Ann Arbor activists attended a SLID convention in New York State. It was there that the organization was renamed Students for a Democratic Society. SDS became famous (in some people's eyes, infamous), producing well-publicized leaders in student-rights and antiwar activities.

"Those were exciting days, for there seemed to be fresh hope for a new world with economic plenty and love between all peoples," Luther recalls wistfully. One evening in the mid-1960s, he and his wife, Joan, entertained several SDS members, including Tom Hayden, who went on to become one of the Chicago Seven (and, briefly, Jane Fonda's second husband). Earlier the couple opened their home to, among others, socialists Norman Thomas and Michael Harrington and civil rights activist John Lewis, later elected to Congress from Georgia and still serving there. Lewis had slept on Luther's floor during the first meeting of SDS, held in Ann Arbor to address discrimination in the North.

Luther's legacy to the co-op movement rests also in his training of generations of co-op student members on how to be good housekeepers, cooks, and bookkeepers. He taught double-entry accounting to hundreds of house treasurers so that they could successfully close their books three times a year, at the end of the fall, winter, and summer terms. He used the skills and resourcefulness he had learned on the farm to help students maintain both the physical appearance and the successful functioning of the houses.

Not that Luther and the co-opers always co-existed in mutual harmony. Many of the students were as strong-willed as he was, and they clashed on issues such as whether or not to purchase a new house. Jim Jones, who followed Luther as ICC student co-op administrator in Ann Arbor, says, "Luther described himself as a coach. He would throw out the ball to the students. He was always willing to step aside and give others the power to deal with things."

Long retired, Luther and Joan still attend annual meetings of the North American Students of Cooperation, held at the Michigan Union. They are the longest-serving co-opers present. At the banquet in the Union ballroom, to everyone's delight, Luther leads the 500 co-opers in songs embodying the ideals of the movement, including a rousing rendition of "I'm my own landlord." Luther served 15,000 co-op members during his thirty-three-year career.

The last of the Buchele brothers to marry, Luther exchanged vows with Joan Bross, a U-M graduate, librarian, and former ICC member, on February 4, 1961, when he was forty. Luther and Joan reared four children: Royd, Theresa, Libbie, and Heidi. In August of 2005, at age eighty-five, Luther became the grandfather of twin boys, born to Libbie and her husband, Eric Hoy. They were named Luther and Wesley! A year later, he and Joan welcomed another grandchild, Alexander Buchele Harris, the son of Heidi and her husband, Michael Harris. In the spring of 2008, Nichole was born to Heidi and Michael, and Libbie and Eric also welcomed a daughter, Sadie. Thus at the age of eighty-eight, Luther is the proud grandfather of five children under the age of three!

A further highlight of Luther's long association with co-ops came in 1987, two years after he retired. He was named by the National Association of Business Cooperatives to the National Cooperative Hall of Fame, in Washington, D.C., and cited as the "father of the student cooperative movement," because the cooperatives he built served as models for those at other universities. Joan, their family, and Wes and Mary attended the celebration.

In childhood and throughout their lives, their neighbors in Cedar Vale called Bessie Buchele's sons "good boys." No wonder: they worked to help their mother keep and maintain the family farm and, with her, survived daunting debt, the hardships of the Depression, and the loss of their father. Each one managed to acquire an education and was successful in his chosen profession. Equally important, these "good boys" were blessed with wonderful wives.

Joan Bross (Luther), Helen Fettig (Paul), Adelma Watson (Matthew), Irma McCollough (Robert), Vergie Bryant (Julian), Mary Jagger (Wesley), and Thelma Noland (Ned).

Speaking at the funeral of Helen, Paul's wife, in February 2008, Nancy Buchele, a daughter of Julian and Vergie's, aptly described all of the Buchele wives as: "very strong, independent women." Mother Bessie had every reason to be proud of her seven sons, their families, and the lives they led.

Thirteen of the twenty-one grandchildren of Charles and Bessie Buchele.

Photographs

The "Buchele Family Farm Home" for over seventy years.

The Big Red Barn before *(above)* and after *(below)* the 1975 tornado.

Joan and Libbie watch the Railroad Company lift the tornado-overturned grain boxcar back on track.

Chas. J. Buchele,

FLOUR, FEED AND GRAIN.

Planet Mills and Elevator—LaFayette, Ind.
Excelsior Mills and Elevator—Bluffton, Ind.

PRESENTED BY — BRANDS OF FLOUR... { "BUCHELE'S GILT EDGE" "GOLD BAND" "GOLDEN WEDDING" }

Upper L: Robert, age 2, promotes his father's "Gilt Edge Flour."
Above: Robert and Ned play in the grass while their mother is laid to rest in a Liberty Center, Ohio, cemetery.
Left: Charles Buchele's business card.

Tall, handsome, and debonair Charles J. Buchele, circa 1911.

Bessie Fisher, Emporia Kansas Teacher's College co-ed, 1902, with her "Gibson Girl" hairstyle.

Aunt Kate Buchele, Aunt Ada Holroyd, and Bessie Fisher wear fancy millinery during their Western trip.

Julian and Paul receive sound farming advice from their older brothers, Ned and Robert.

Luther and daughters Libbie and Heidi ride cowboy horses on a visit to the Buchele Bros. Farm.

Luther milking.

Counting cattle.

Julian on grain combine unloading wheat into a truck.

Large round bales of hay lying in fields make pleasant rural scenes along the world's highways and byways.

Innovative Baler

Farmers were saved from the backbreaking chore of slinging hay bales in the 1960s when Iowa State agricultural engineering professor Wesley Buchele and a group of student researchers invented a baler that produced large, round bales that could be moved by tractor. The baler has become the predominant forage-handling machine in the United States.

Historical plaque in front of ISU Ag. Eng. building to honor the large round bale baler inventors.

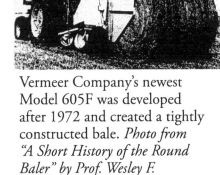

Vermeer Company's newest Model 605F was developed after 1972 and created a tightly constructed bale. *Photo from "A Short History of the Round Baler" by Prof. Wesley F. Buchele, ISU Ag. Eng. Dept.*

Prof. Wesley Buchele and student Virgil Haverdink, the co-inventors of the large round baler. Pat.#3,534,537 10-20-70.

Wesley marvels at all those big round bales as if they were his children.

Helical-flow threshing cone invented by Wesley F. Buchele, Ph.D., in 1952 at ISU. He was granted two U.S. Patents. Helical-flow threshing cylinders are in all U.S.A. combines. China uses ten million hand-fed cone rice threshers.

Wesley in Japan.

Three of 30 Holstein milk cows.

Matthew in New Guinea.

Combining alfalfa seed near the farmstead.

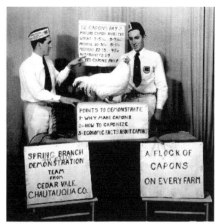

4-H Clubbers Luther *(left)* & Wesley demonstrate "How to Make a Capon."

Co-op logos.

Organized in 1939, Jay Hawk House was the first student co-op on the K.U. Campus.

Twin Pines Co-op logo painted on the "Big U Rock" at Hill and Washtenaw Streets. *Photo by Joan Buchele.*

Luther Buchele *(right front)* and members of the K.U. Rock Chalk Co-op.

Card game at the I.C.C. Michigan Co-op.

House officers at
I.C.C. Vail Co-op.

Luther receives the Cooperative
Hall of Fame award from Ben
Franklin, portrayed by an actor.
Franklin, who receieved the same
award, organized the first U.S.A.
Mutual Fire Insurance Society,
which protects its members' homes
from total financial loss in case
of fire.

Folk singing à la Pete Seeger at the
I.C.C. Robert Owen Co-op in
the early fifties.

Left: Coopers at the I.C.C.
North Campus Co-op prepare
the evening meal for fifty
members.